A Journey Through THE HUMAN BODY

by Steve Parker

Illustrated by John Haslam

QEB

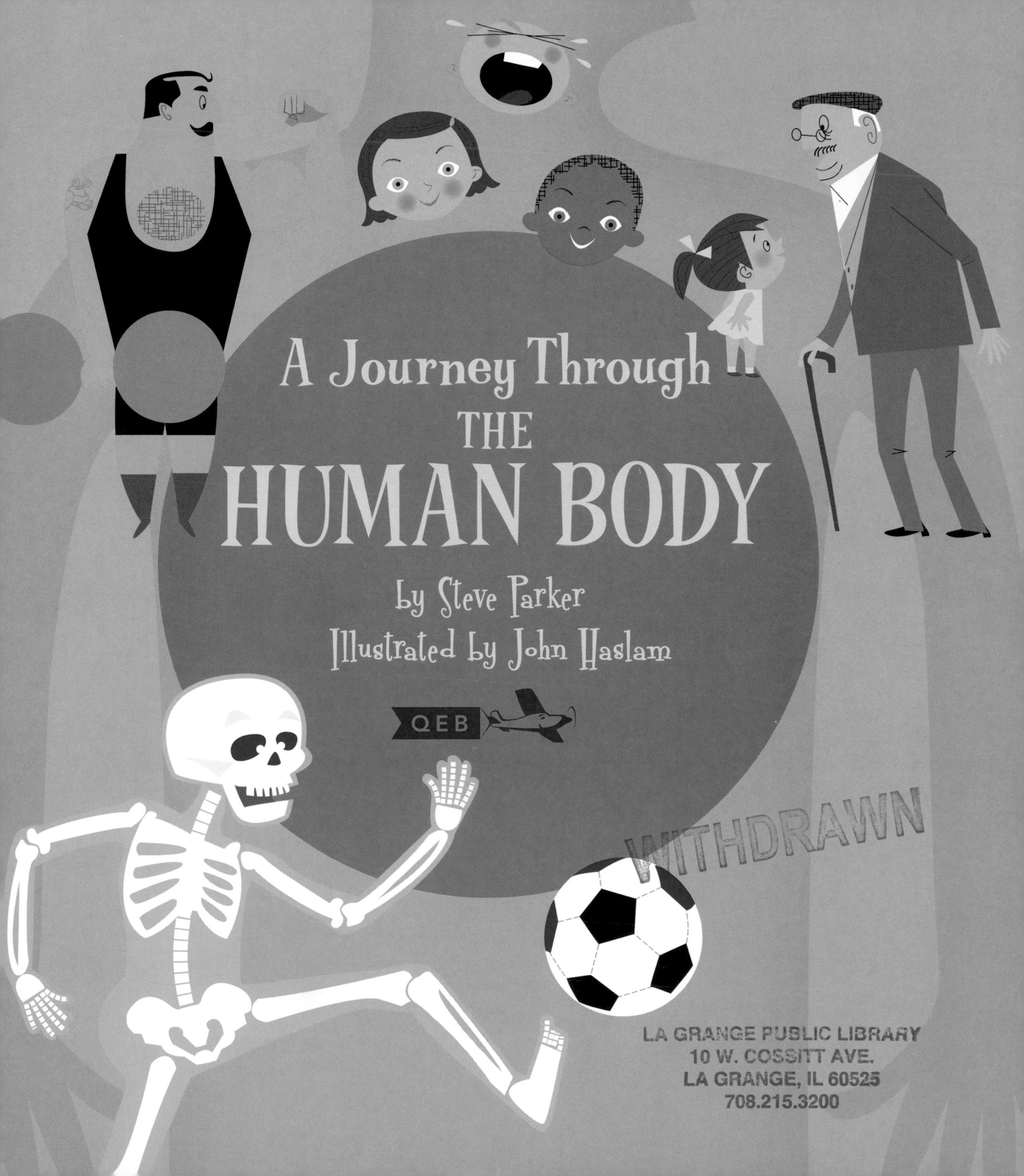

Part of The Quarto Group
The Old Brewery, 6 Blundell Street,
London, N7 9BH

First published in the UK in 2015 by QED Publishing

Published in the United States in 2015 by
QEB Publishing, Inc.
2 Wrigley, Suite A
Irvine, CA 92618

A CIP record for this book is available from the Library of Congress.

ISBN 978 1 60992 827 8

Publisher: Zeta Jones
Associate Publisher: Maxime Boucknooghe
Art Director: Susi Martin
Managing Editor: Laura Knowles
Production: Nikki Ingram
Consultant: Michael Bright

Originated in Hong Kong by Cypress Colours (HK) Ltd
Printed and bound in China by Toppan Leefung Printing Ltd.

10 9 8 7 6 5 4 3 2 1 15 16 17 18 19

Contents

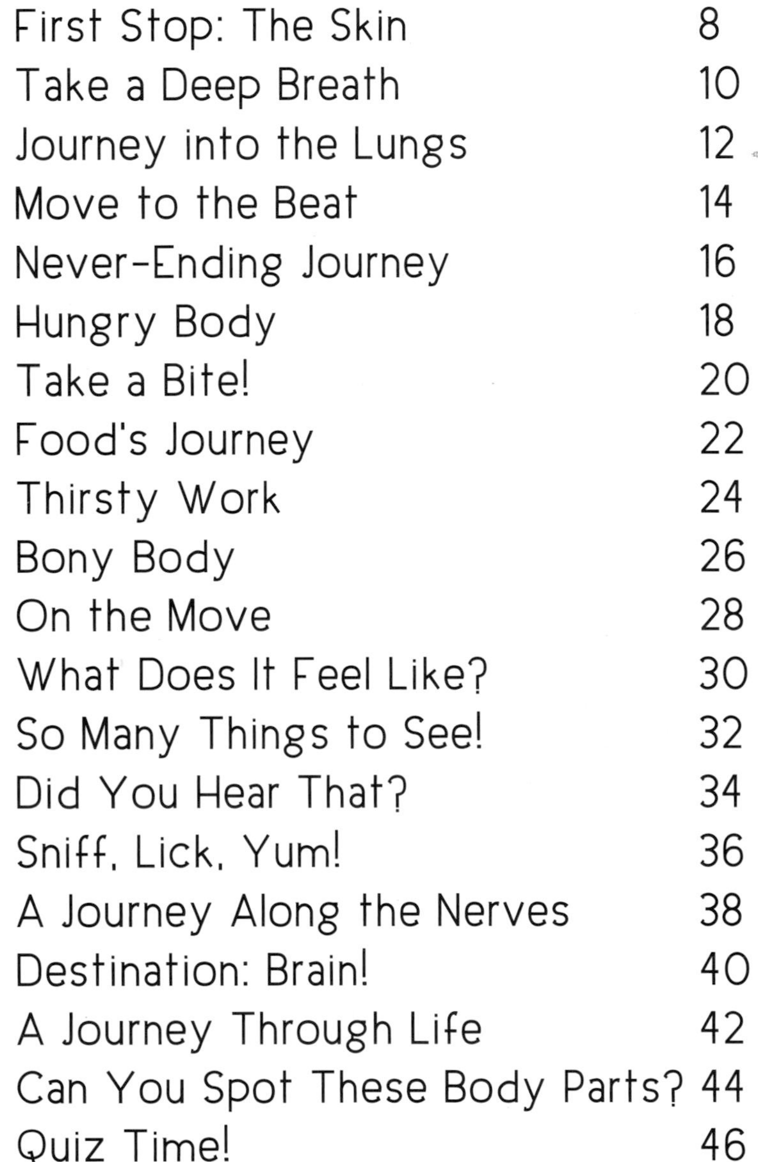

Let's Begin Our Journey

Where shall we go on our journey today? Let's explore one of the most amazing things in the whole world. What is it? To find out, take a look in a mirror...

...It's you! In some ways, your body is like many other animal bodies. You have two eyes, two ears, a nose, and mouth. Inside, you have a heart, blood, bones, and a brain. You eat and breathe and move.

In other ways, your body is different. You have no tail. You walk on two legs. You have fingers that can hold even tiny things. You are not covered in fur, feathers, or scales.

We Are All Different

Look at all the people around you. Every human body is slightly different. Some people are tall, others are not so tall. Some are wide, others are slimmer.

Some skin is smooth. Other skin has creases and wrinkles. Skin color ranges from light to dark.

Hair comes in many colors—silver, blonde, red, brown, black!

Some people have wavy or curly hair, and others have straight hair.

There are all shades of eye color, from pale blue and green to dark brown.

What a wonderful bunch of people!

First Stop: The Skin

Every time you touch something, put on clothes, or dry with a towel, tiny bits of skin fall off! But skin never wears out, because new skin is always growing underneath.

Skin stretches over your fingers, elbows, and other joints. It mends cuts and scrapes on its own. It is amazing stuff!

Your hair grows by the width of your finger every month. Nails grow much more slowly—they take four months to grow that much. Both need a trim now and then.

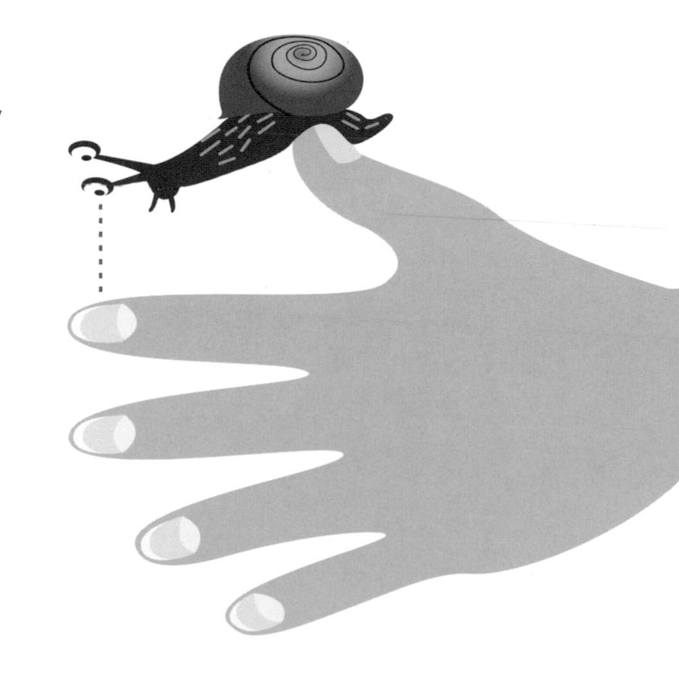

Skin and nails need to be washed often. No one wants to be dirty and smelly, or to spread germs that can make you ill.

Take a Deep Breath!

Puff, pant! Your body always has to breathe. It needs something called oxygen to stay alive. Luckily, there's plenty of oxygen in the air.

Air goes through your nose and mouth and down your throat. It carries on along a tube called the windpipe, traveling deep into your chest and into parts called lungs.

Breathe in

But how does air get down into the lungs? Breathing in happens when muscles between your rib bones and under your chest work to make the chest bigger. This sucks in fresh air.

To breathe out, the muscles go relaxed and floppy and the old air is pushed out. When your body is doing something active, like running or swimming, it needs more oxygen. So it breathes faster and deeper.

Journey into the Lungs

Deep in the chest are two spongy lungs. They are full of tiny bags, like mini-balloons. These are known as alveoli. Each one is so small, there are hundreds of millions of them in each lung.

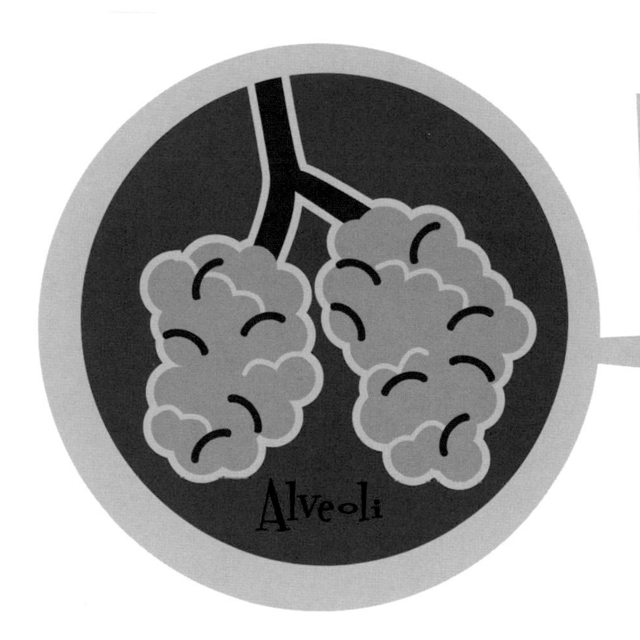

Air from outside the body ends up in the alveoli. Here, the oxygen in the air moves through to blood that is in tiny tubes all around the alvioli. The tubes are thinner than a hair and are called capillaries.

Blood coming into the lungs does not have much oxygen. It's been used up around the body.

When the blood travels to the lungs, it gets oxygen from the air in the alveoli. Then it flows away, taking this oxygen all around the body.

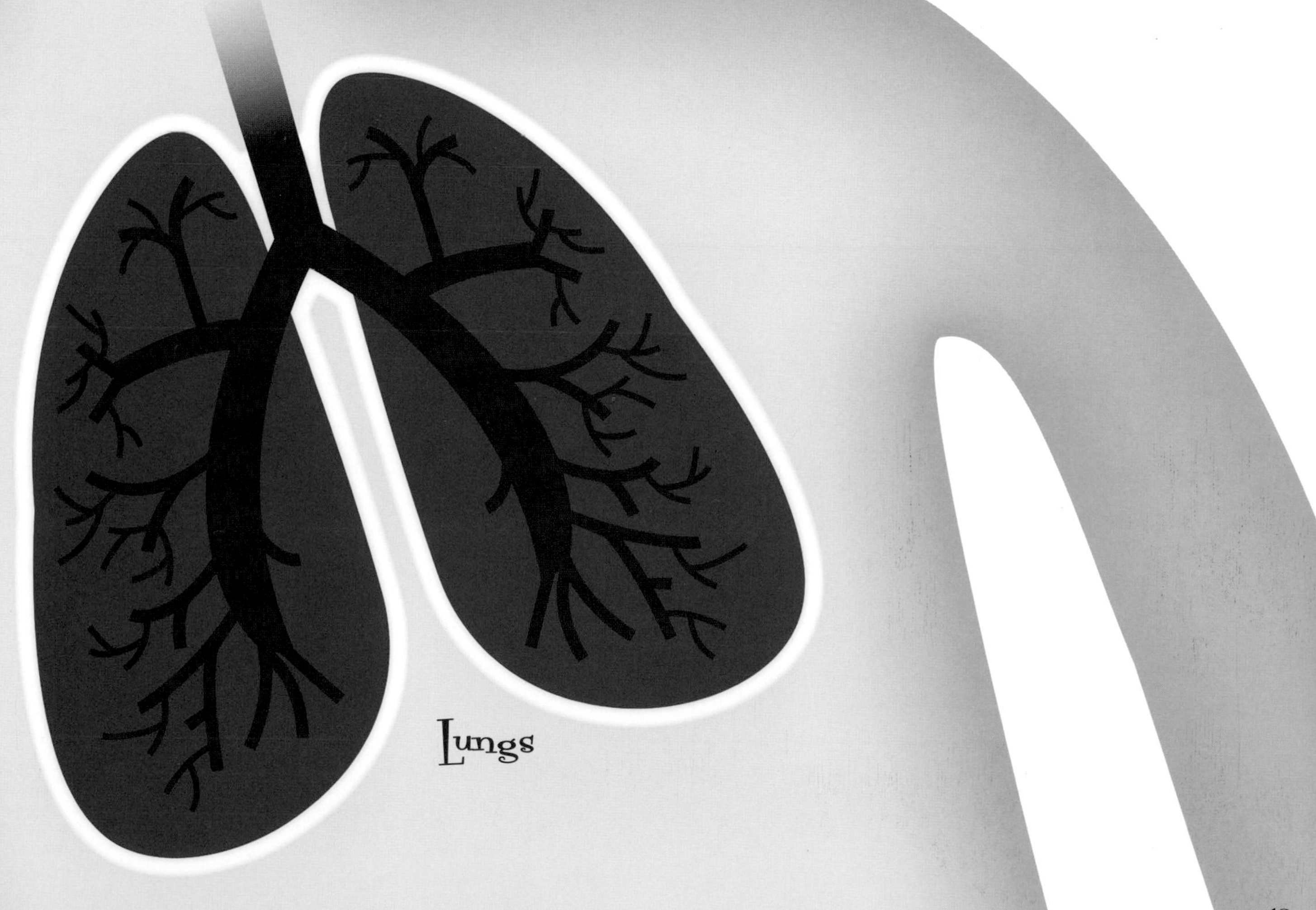

Move to the Beat

Thump, thump... thump, thump! You don't just breathe faster when you run and jump around. Your heart beats faster, too. Have you ever felt it thumping in your chest?

Your heart is between your two lungs. It is like a bag of strong muscle. The muscles squeeze to make blood from inside the heart flow out into tubes that go to your other body parts.

Each squeeze is called a heartbeat. After a heartbeat, the heart fills with more blood. Usually the heart beats slowly, about once each second. But if the body's muscles are busy, they need more energy and oxygen, carried by the blood. So the heart beats faster, more than twice each second.

Thumping, thumping, the heart keeps pumping!

Never-Ending Journey

Blood carries everything your body needs. It contains oxygen from your lungs. It also has nutrients from food, for moving and growing.

Blood is always on the move. It is pushed around your body by the beats of your heart.

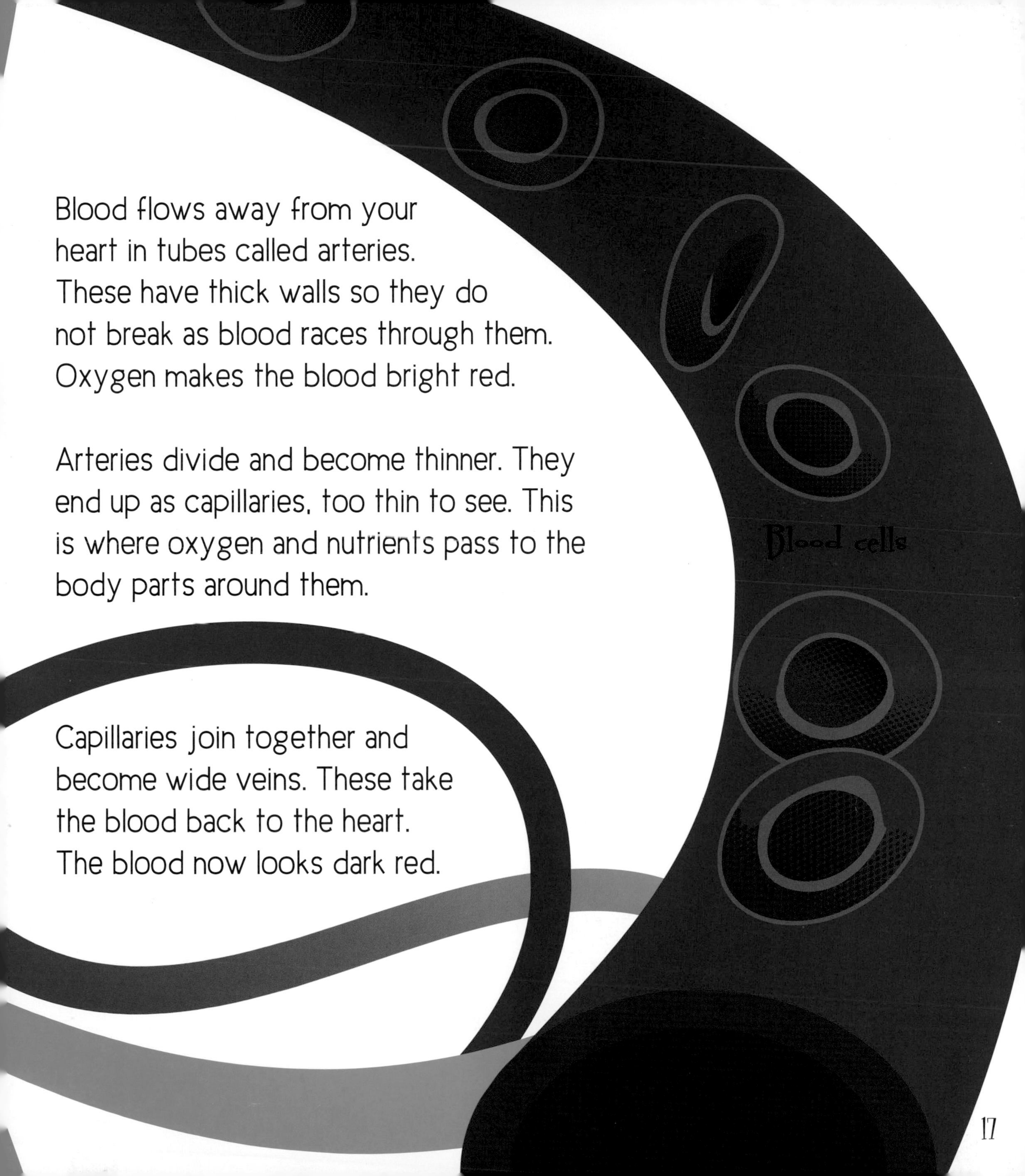

Blood flows away from your heart in tubes called arteries. These have thick walls so they do not break as blood races through them. Oxygen makes the blood bright red.

Arteries divide and become thinner. They end up as capillaries, too thin to see. This is where oxygen and nutrients pass to the body parts around them.

Capillaries join together and become wide veins. These take the blood back to the heart. The blood now looks dark red.

Hungry Body

Moving, running around, talking, sleeping—phew! They all use energy. This is one reason your body needs food. Another reason is to get nutrients to grow bigger, and to make new parts for old.

Sweets should be a treat. Don't eat too many!

It's best for your body if you eat lots of different foods. Fruits and vegetables have lots of nutrients and are tasty and healthy. Bread, rice, and pasta give you energy. Eating a small amount of meat and fish is good for you, too. Your body also needs plenty of water and other drinks, especially when it's hot.

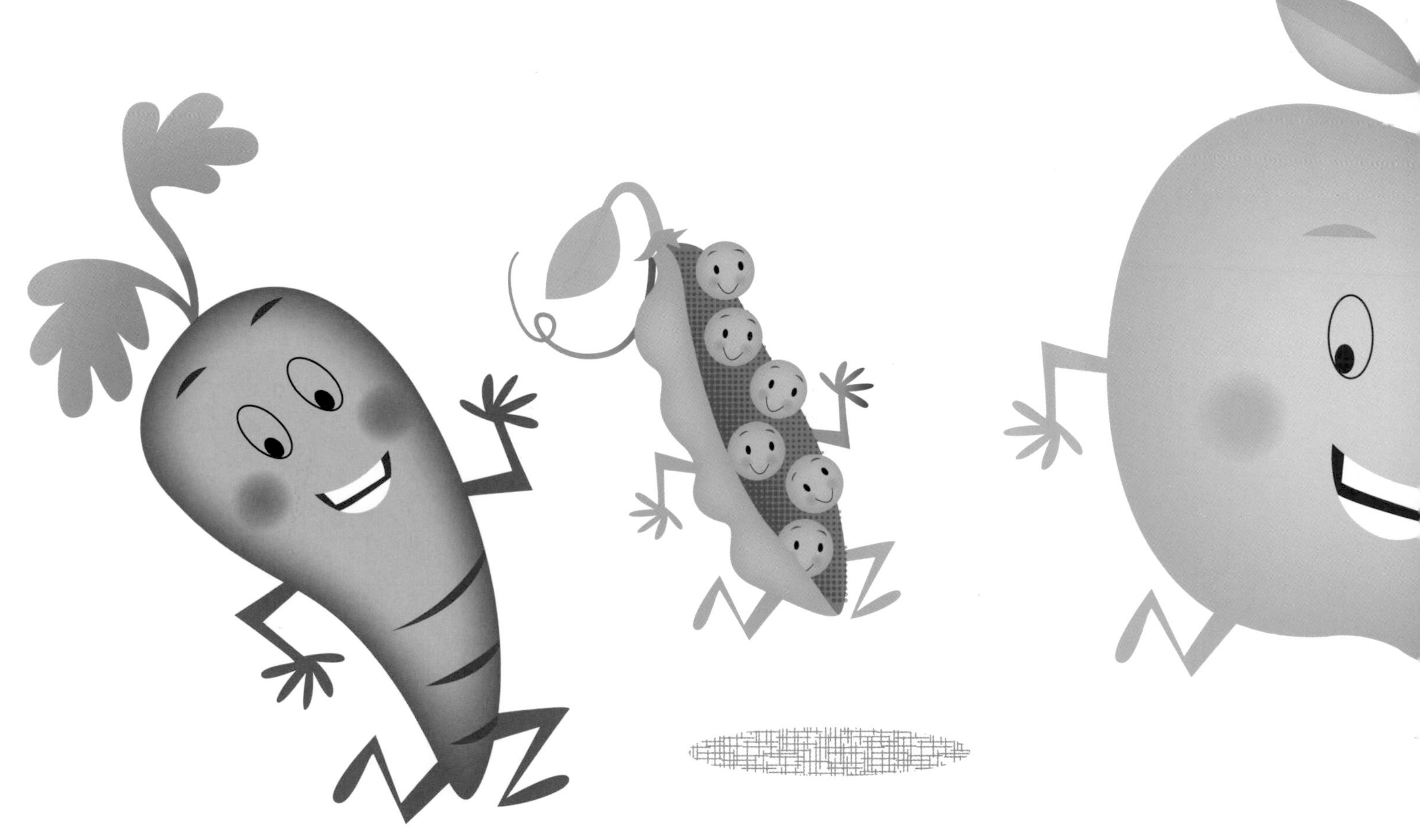

Eat your greens to keep healthy...

Take a Bite!

Your body likes you to eat slowly. Food needs to be chewed so it is soft and easy to swallow. If you rush, your food could go down the wrong way, into the breathing tubes, which is very dangerous.

Teeth are the hardest parts of your body. The front ones are thin and sharp to bite and slice. The back ones are wide and bumpy to squash and crush.

The teeth you grow as a baby will fall out, and a bigger set of grown-up teeth will take their place. After that, no more can grow. That's why it is so important to brush your teeth after meals and before bedtime, and never miss a visit to the dentist.

Food's Journey

When you swallow food, its first stop is the stomach. This stretchy bag squeezes the food and adds strong juices to it. The juices break food down into smaller pieces.

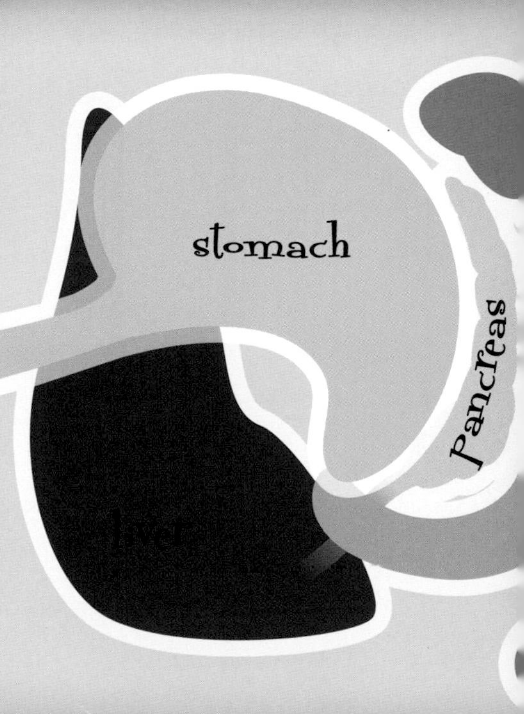

The next part of the journey is through a long, thin tube called the small intestine, which is curled and coiled into the middle of the body.

Inside the small intenstine, food is broken down more. The nutrients and the energy, in the form of body sugars, pass into the blood.

After this long tube comes a wider one, the large intestine. It takes in a few more nutrients and also water.

All that is left are brown, smelly lumps, ready to come out the other end. Can you guess what they are?

Thirsty Work

Every body needs a regular drink. Water or fruit juices are great. When the weather is hot, and after lots of action, your body needs even more to drink.

Water from drinks goes into the blood. This is important because water is always being taken out of the blood, by two parts called kidneys. They need the water to get rid of wastes that blood collects from all around the body.

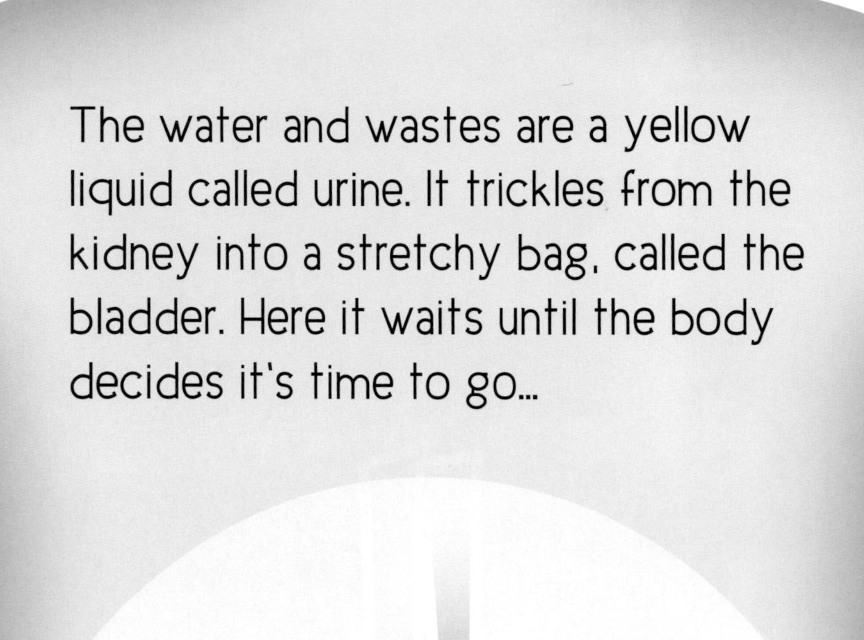

The water and wastes are a yellow liquid called urine. It trickles from the kidney into a stretchy bag, called the bladder. Here it waits until the body decides it's time to go...

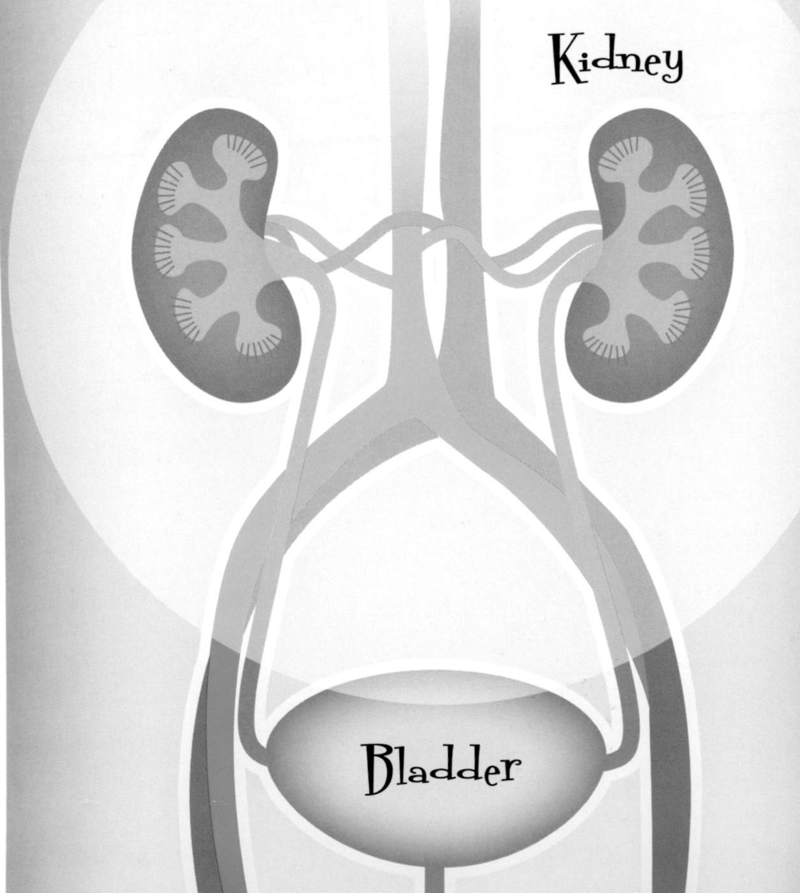

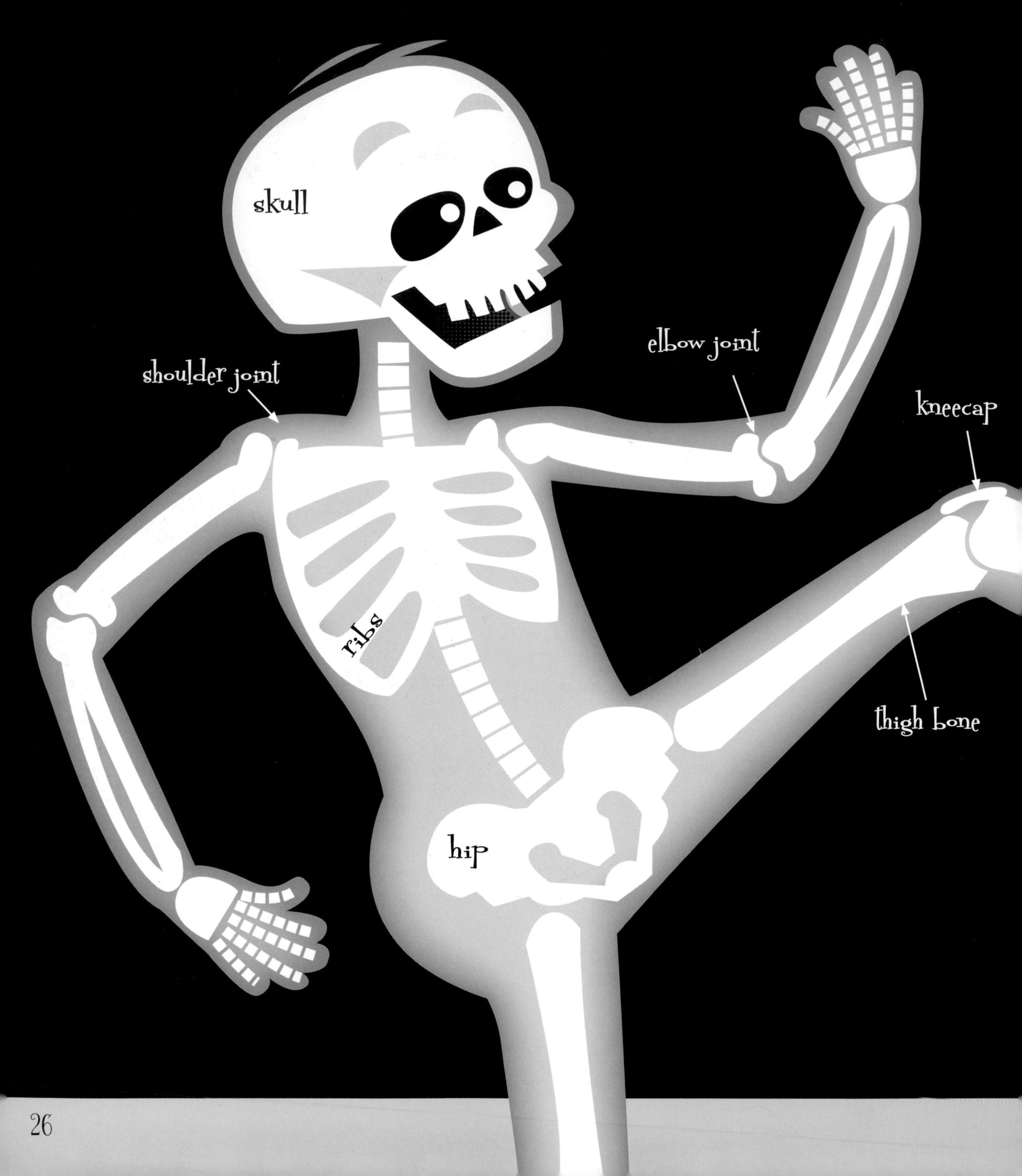
skull
shoulder joint
elbow joint
kneecap
ribs
thigh bone
hip

Bony Body

Time to get going again. Your body can stand, run, jump, and lift because of its bones, muscles, and joints. There are 206 bones, each one hard and strong. Together they form the skeleton.

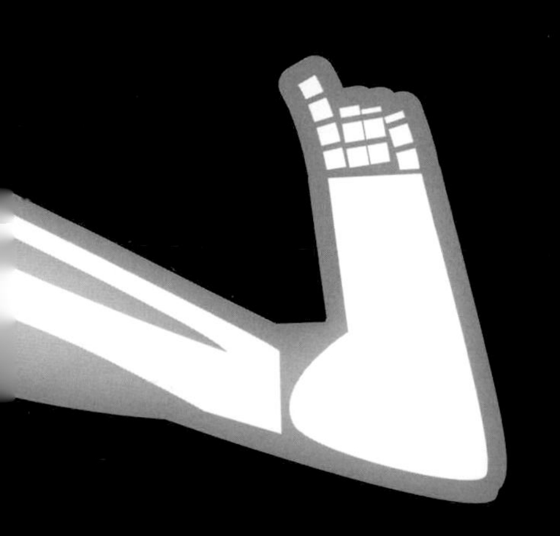

The skull bones protect the brain and make up the face and jaw. One of the tiny ear bones is as small as this "U." The rib bones guard the heart and lungs. The longest is the thigh bone. It's one-quarter of the body's height!

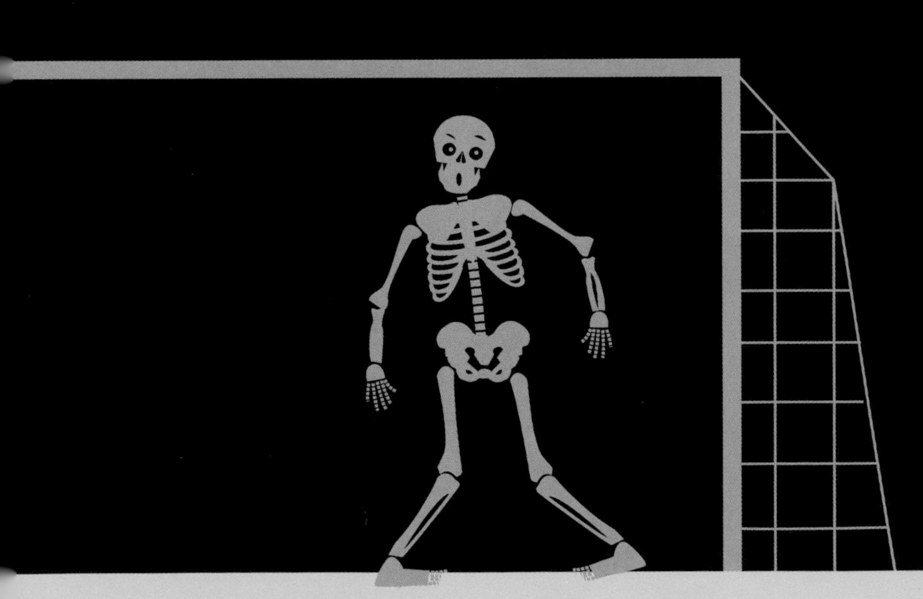

On the Move

Without muscles, your body wouldn't be able to move at all. Muscles are in the heart, stomach, and intestines. They are all around the bones of the skeleton, too, making the body's every movement.

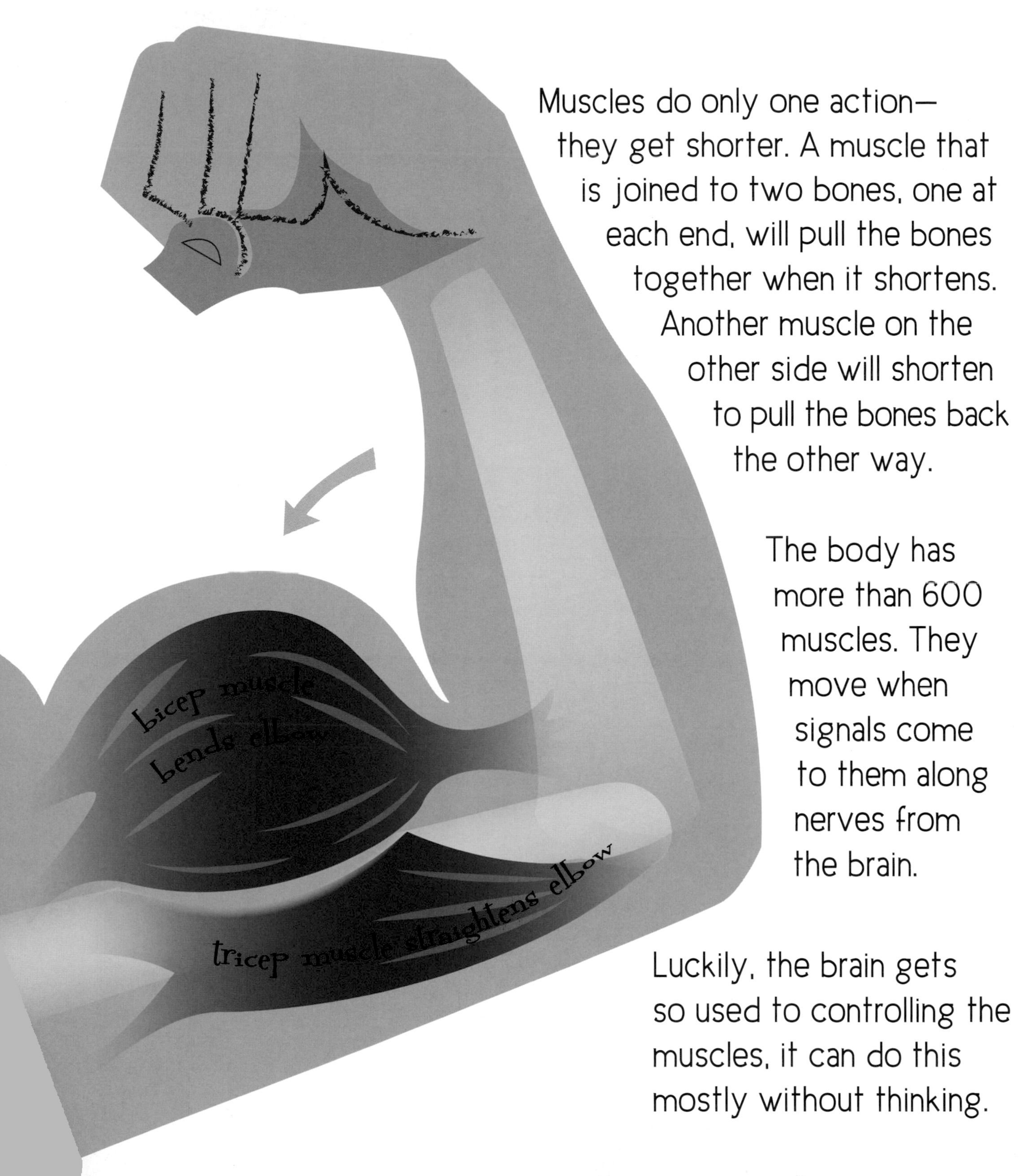

Muscles do only one action—they get shorter. A muscle that is joined to two bones, one at each end, will pull the bones together when it shortens. Another muscle on the other side will shorten to pull the bones back the other way.

The body has more than 600 muscles. They move when signals come to them along nerves from the brain.

Luckily, the brain gets so used to controlling the muscles, it can do this mostly without thinking.

What Does It Feel Like?

Your body finds out about the world by using its senses. These include seeing, hearing, smell, taste, and touch.

Your skin can feel many different things. A cup is hard, smooth, and dry. The water inside is sloshy, cold, and wet.

Your skin is sensitive to the tiniest touches, like a pet mouse's tiny feet, and even a feather tickling your skin.

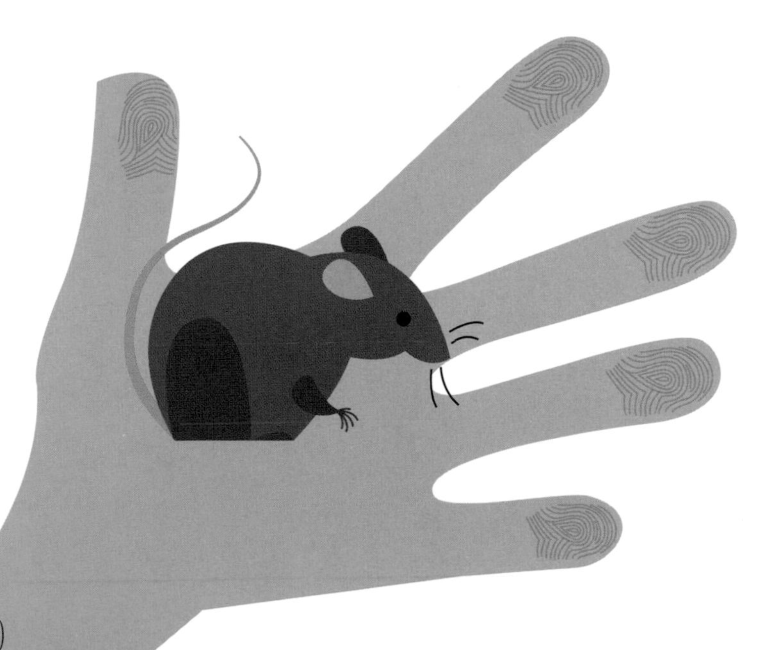

But how does skin feel all these things? Thousands of tiny patches in your skin, too small to see, feel hot or cold, hard or soft, wet or dry, smooth or bumpy. They send these feelings all the way to your brain, as something we call "nerve signals."

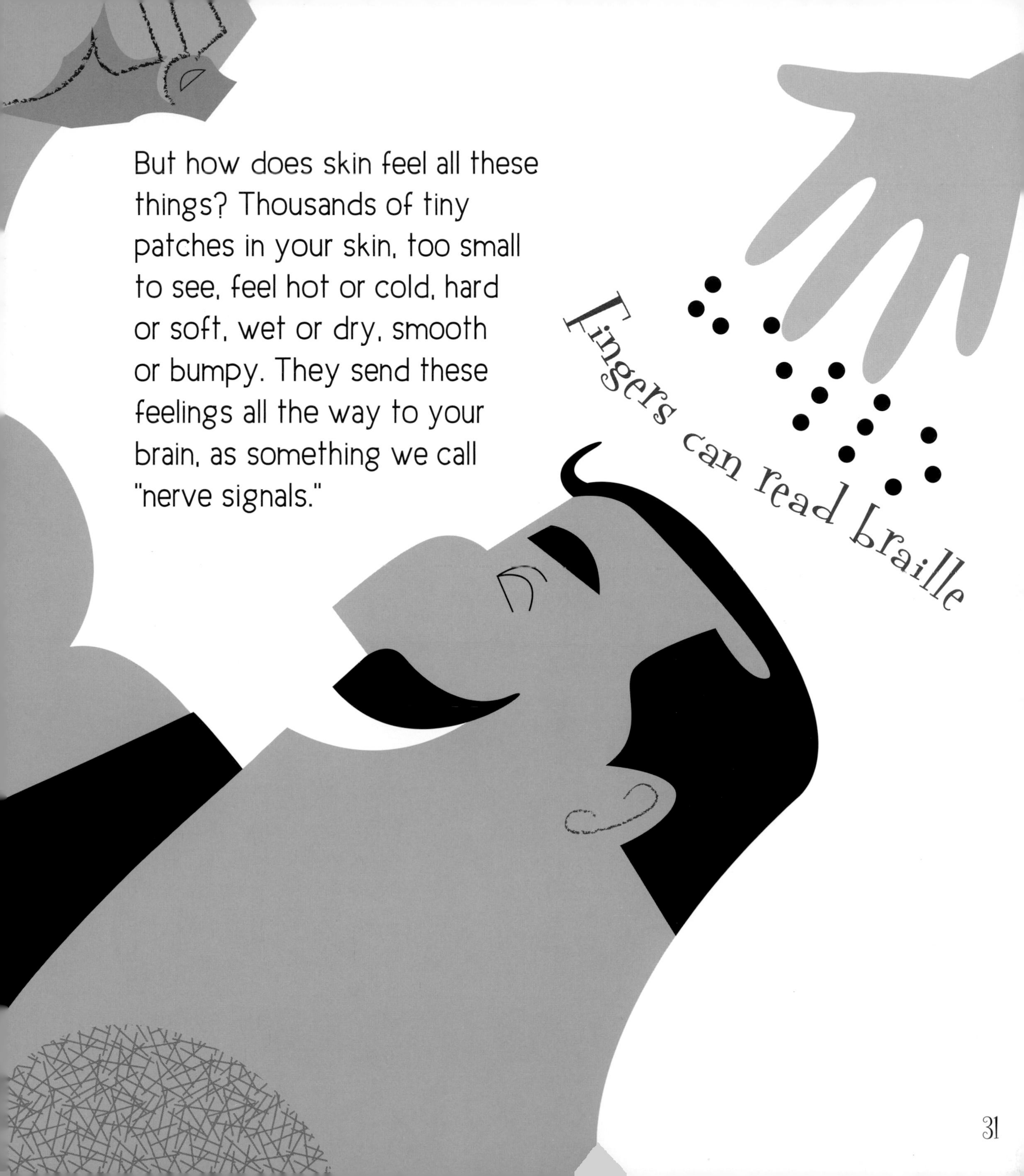

So Many Things To See!

Eyes do the seeing. Light goes into the dark hole, the pupil, in the colored part of the eye. The light shines onto the inside back of the eye, the retina. This makes tiny pieces of electricity, called nerve signals, which go to the brain.

In bright light, the pupil gets smaller. This stops too much light from getting into the eye and causing harm.

The eyelids protect the outside of the eye. They close quickly, or blink, every few seconds to wipe away dust and germs.

eardrum
cochlea
tiny bones

Did You Hear That?

Ears are not just the curly flaps on the sides of your head. Each flap carries sounds into a short tunnel that ends at a thin, bouncy piece of skin, the eardrum.

Sounds shake the eardrum. This shakes three tiny bones next to it. The bones shake the next part, the cochlea, which is shaped like a snail. The cochlea makes nerve signals for the brain.

Sniff, Lick, Yum!

Smell is sensed by the nose. Tiny specks of smell substances, much too small to see, float in the air. The nose breathes them in. They touch the inside lining, which makes nerve signals for the brain. There are more than a trillion different smells!

Taste is sensed by the mouth. Like smell, there are tiny specks of taste substances—too small to see—in food and drink. When they touch the tongue, it makes nerve signals that go to the brain.

A Journey Along the Nerves

The body is alive with tiny bursts of electricity called nerve signals. They go along nerves, which are like bendy wires. The signals travel fast, from head to toe in less than one-tenth of a second.

Some nerve signals start in the brain. They go along nerves to muscles, to control the body's movements.

Other nerve signals start in the sense parts like the eyes and ears. They go the other way, to the brain. This is how the brain knows what is happening all around.

There are thousands of nerves, and millions of nerve signals every second. They are like the body's own Internet.

Destination: Brain!

The brain is the most important part of the body. It is the place for thoughts, feelings, worries, happiness, deciding, and remembering.

Some parts of your brain are used for thinking, planning, and making decisions. They also store memories that last a short time, such as what you had for breakfast today.

Other parts of your brain are used to help with movement, seeing, hearing, smell, taste, and touch.

Strong feelings like hunger, thirst, fear, anger, joy, and love all happen deep inside your brain. This is also where you make memories that last a long time.

A Journey Through Life

All bodies start as babies. They cannot do much except feed on milk, sleep, and often cry! With lots of care, they grow well and start to eat their own food.

Babies grow into toddlers. At first they crawl, then they walk in a wobbly way. Soon they start to run and jump—and talk, too.

Toddlers grow into children. They learn all kinds of things, like how to get dressed, wash, draw, write, go to school, and stay safe. They learn more and more about the world.

By about 20 years old, the body stops getting bigger. It is now a grown-up!

Grown-up bodies can have their own children and make a bigger family. That means new bodies to grow up and have their own amazing journeys!

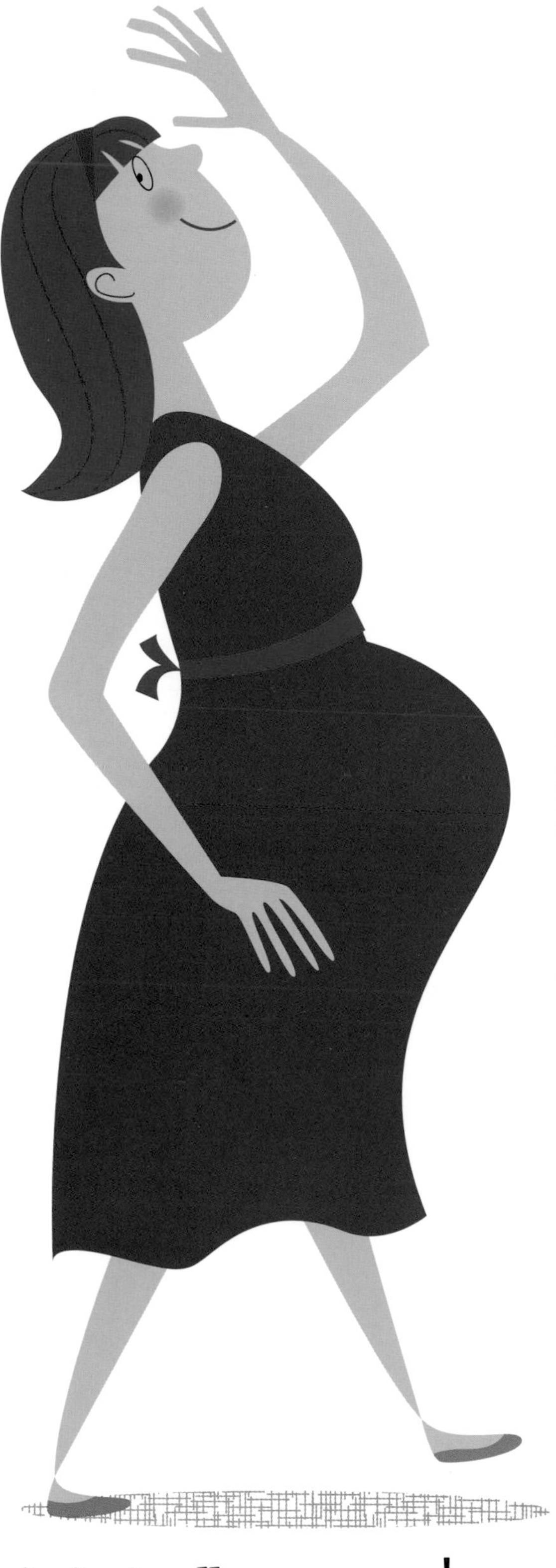

Teenager

Grown–up

...and it starts all over again!

Can You Spot These Body Parts?

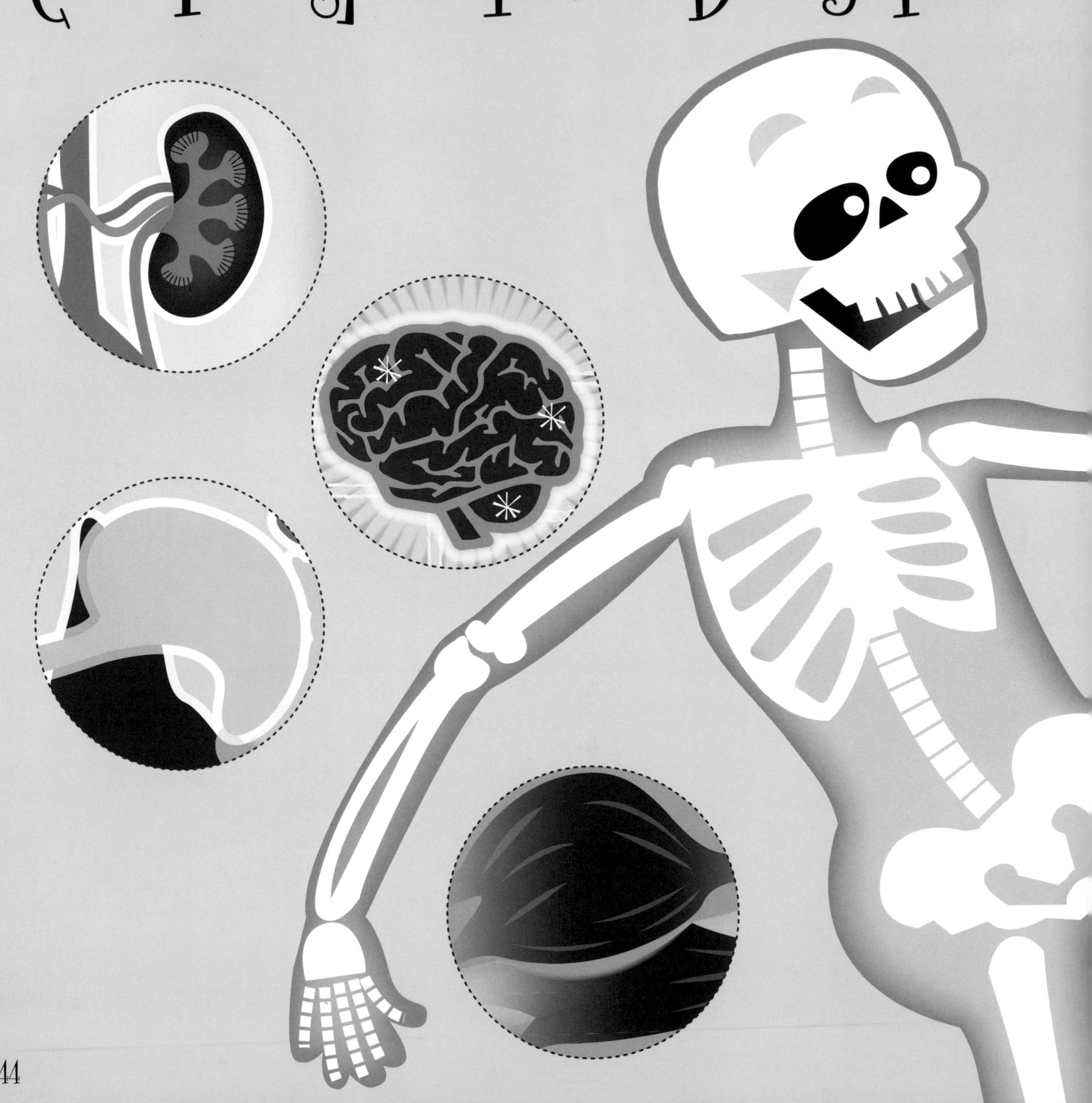

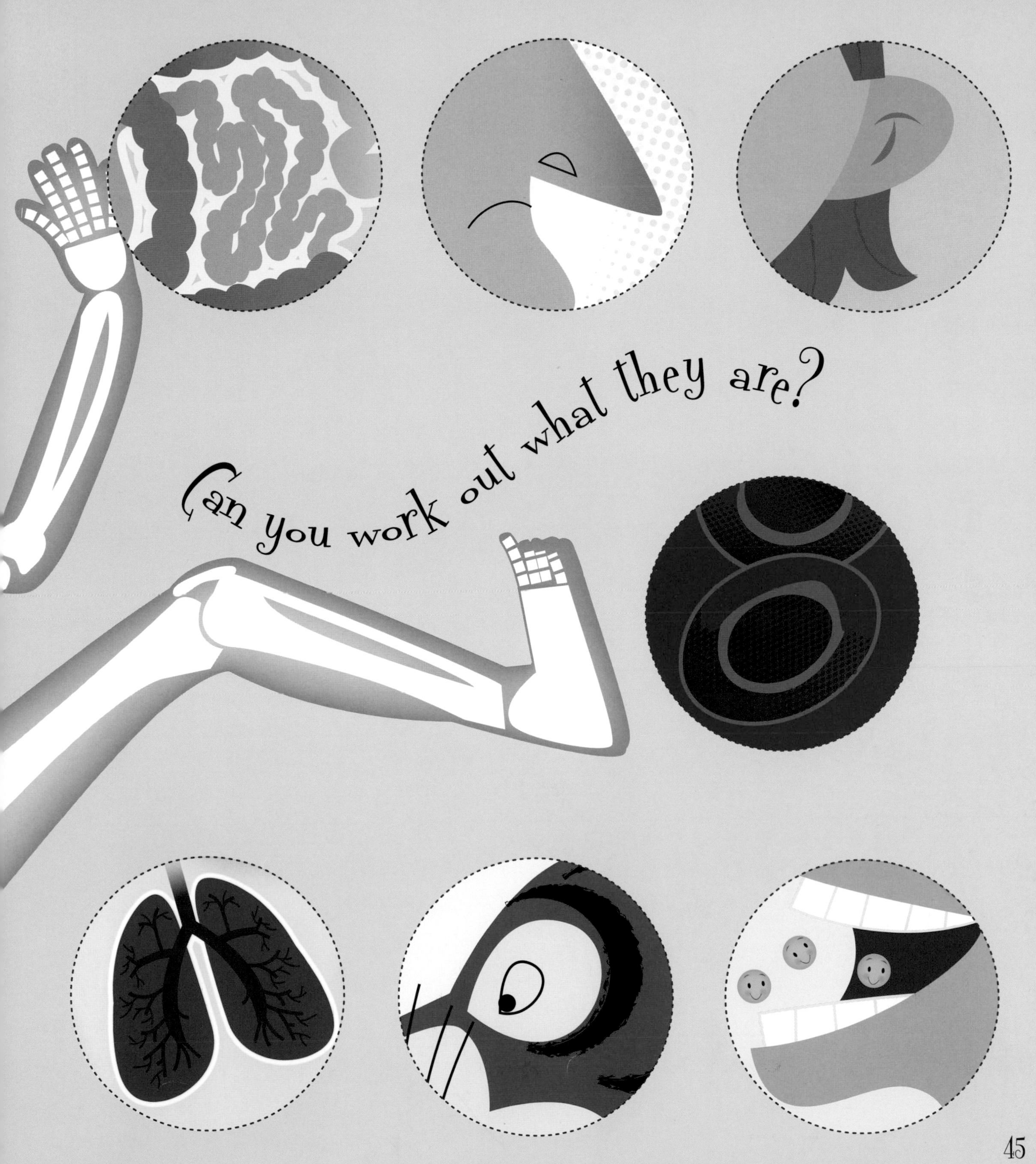
Can you work out what they are?

Quiz Time!

Can you answer these questions about the human body? Here's a hint—you can find all the answers in this book.

1. Which grows more slowly, hair or nails?

2. What body part helps you to smell?

3. What does your body need to breathe?

4. Which body part is used for thinking?

5. What body part pumps blood around your body?

6. Where in your body is your eardrum?

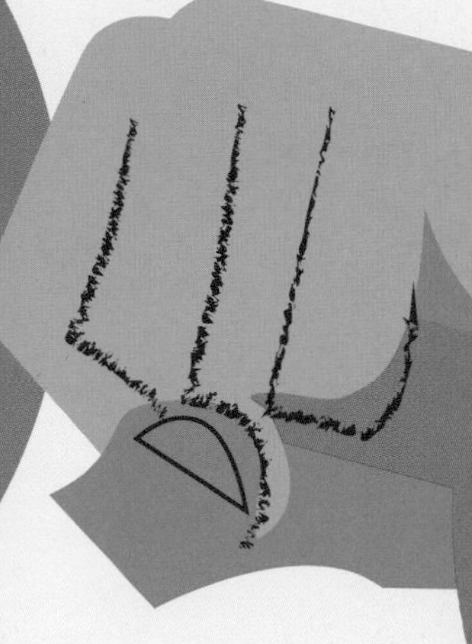

7. Where does your food go after you swallow it?

8. What is the hardest part of your body?

Answers

1. Nails, 2. Your nose, 3. Oxygen from the air, 4. Your brain, 5. Your heart, 6. Your ear, 7. Your stomach, 8. Your teeth.